That's

Ants
Are FARMERS!
And other Strange facts

GARY SPROTT

Rourke
Educational Media

A Division of
Carson
Dellosa
Education

rourkeeducationalmedia.com

Before Reading: *Building Background Knowledge and Vocabulary*

Building background knowledge can help children process new information and build upon what they already know. Before reading a book, it is important to tap into what children already know about the topic. This will help them develop their vocabulary and increase their reading comprehension.

Questions and Activities to Build Background Knowledge:

1. Look at the front cover of the book and read the title. What do you think this book will be about?
2. What do you already know about this topic?
3. Take a book walk and skim the pages. Look at the table of contents, photographs, captions, and bold words. Did these text features give you any information or predictions about what you will read in this book?

Vocabulary: *Vocabulary Is Key to Reading Comprehension*

Use the following directions to prompt a conversation about each word.

- Read the vocabulary words.
- What comes to mind when you see each word?
- What do you think each word means?

> **Vocabulary Words:**
> - camouflage
> - catapult
> - colonies
> - host
> - inconspicuous
> - venomous

During Reading: *Reading for Meaning and Understanding*

To achieve deep comprehension of a book, children are encouraged to use close reading strategies. During reading, it is important to have children stop and make connections. These connections result in deeper analysis and understanding of a book.

 Close Reading a Text

During reading, have children stop and talk about the following:

- Any confusing parts
- Any unknown words
- Text to text, text to self, text to world connections
- The main idea in each chapter or heading

Encourage children to use context clues to determine the meaning of any unknown words. These strategies will help children learn to analyze the text more thoroughly as they read.

When you are finished reading this book, turn to the next-to-last page for **After Reading Questions** and an **Activity**.

Table of Contents

Assassins to Zombies

They're everywhere. Under your feet and above your head. In your house and around your garden. They're hunters, farmers, builders, and cold-blooded killers. They're insects! The world of these creepers, crawlers, and fliers will leave you bug-eyed with wonder.

dragonfly

Heard the Buzz?

Insects are the world's largest and most diverse group of animals. Scientists have identified about one million species of insects but believe there could be millions more!

mantis

Assassin bugs have a cool trick to confuse predators. These killers stab ants with their beaks, paralyze them with poisonous spit, and suck out their fluids. The assassin bug then piles the dead ants on its back as **camouflage** to hide from jumping spiders and other attackers.

camouflage (KAM-uh-flahzh): coloring or covering that makes animals, people, and objects look like their surroundings

Bloodsucking mosquitoes have a sneaky, lowdown way to avoid becoming a red splotch under your slapping hand. These annoying buzzers can sense body odors and, well, our feet can be pretty stinky. So, they head south. Unless you have arms like an orangutan, it's not easy to swat a skeeter all the way down there!

Countess Dracula!

Only female mosquitoes drink blood. They use their funnel-like mouths to stab into their victims. Males are pretty much vegetarians—they prefer a nice sip of plant juice!

Like an evil mastermind, the jewel wasp turns cockroaches into zombies! The wasp injects its victim with mind-controlling venom, leads it by its antennae to a nest, and lays an egg on the roach. When the baby wasp hatches, it eats its **host** alive!

 **host** (hohst): an animal or plant from which a parasite gets nutrition

Hi-Yah!

Some roaches defend themselves against jewel wasps with karate! The cockroach lifts itself up and kicks out its legs, which are covered with tiny spikes. Hey, if you have six legs, you might as well use them!

The puss caterpillar is a furry little critter that looks kind of like a curled-up kitten. But, make no mistake, this is no pussycat! Hidden among all that hair are toxic spikes that deliver a painful sting. The most **venomous** caterpillar in the United States, this puss puts the "Ow!" in meow!

venomous (VEN-uh-muhs): full of venom, a toxic substance produced by some animals and plants

A Bitter Bite!

The monarch butterfly's beautiful orange, white, and black markings are a warning to hungry predators: Eat me and you'll get sick! In the caterpillar stage, monarchs feed only on milkweed, a poisonous plant that turns them toxic.

Causing a Stink

You think your chores are tough? Try rolling a giant ball of poop around all day! The dung beetle has a scoop-shaped head—yes, a pooper scooper—and gathers manure from animals such as elephants. It rolls the dung into a ball that it uses as (yuck!) food or (double yuck!) a dwelling.

Strongman, Meet Strongbug!

Don't get into a tug-of-war match with a dung beetle, which has been crowned the world's strongest insect! Some male beetles can pull more than one thousand times their own body weight. That would be like an average man pulling a couple of humpback whales!

Termites are famous for their destructive appetites. Termite **colonies** can eat their way through homes and other structures. But these insects may also be the greatest builders on the planet! Using soil, spit, and poop, termites construct mounds as tall as a giraffe. Some mounds in Brazil are nearly 4,000 years old and were built about the same time as the ancient pyramids of Egypt!

colonies (KAH-luh-neez): large groups of animals that live together

One guess how the stinkbug got its name. Too easy! Only about the size of your fingernail, the stinkbug releases a foul-smelling odor that makes it an unappetizing meal.

Winged Destroyer

The stinkbug's stench defense means it has few natural predators. That's a problem for farmers. The bug is a big eater and can fly as far as 75 miles (121 kilometers) in a day, munching through crops of fruits, vegetables, and nuts.

Mini Mighty Marvels

Ants have been farming for tens of millions of years—far longer than humans have been around! The leafcutter ants of Central and South America bite off pieces of forest plants, but not for eating. The ants use the vegetation like a fertilizer to grow a fungus. That's what these tiny gardeners eat!

Time to Milk the Tiny Cows!

Herder ants are the dairy farmers of the insect world. These ants keep herds of aphids, tiny bugs that suck plant sap and release a sugary liquid called honeydew. The ants milk the aphids by tickling them with their antennae! "Okay, okay, you can have some!"

With a life span of only a few months, grasshoppers don't have time to hang around. At the first sign of danger, they're—boing!—gone. Grasshoppers store energy in their powerful hind legs so they can **catapult** themselves away from predators. They can jump up to 20 times their body length!

 **catapult** (KAT-uh-puhlt): to throw or launch something far over an obstacle

A bee's wings are small compared to its body. It beats its wings more than 200 times a second to stay aloft! But that doesn't stop these busy buzzers from soaring. Bumblebees can fly as high as 29,500 feet (8,992 meters). That's high enough for a bee's-eye view of the top of Mount Everest, the world's tallest peak!

A Meal Fit for a Queen!

In a bee colony, the queen is the boss. She has only one task: Lay eggs. Lots and lots of eggs. When a queen dies, worker bees pick a young female and feed it a food known as royal jelly. This special diet transforms the chosen bee into the colony's new ruler!

Strange as it seems, water scorpions aren't great swimmers. These insects hang out in the mud and muck at the bottom of ponds. The water scorpion grabs fish, beetles, and tadpoles with its two front legs, which look like curved swords. It has two long, thin, tail-like tubes that it raises above the surface to breathe—a butt snorkel!

Row, Row, Row Your Bug!

The water boatman has a flat body and long rear legs that look like oars on a rowboat. This lighter-than-water bug can cruise along the surface of streams. If the boatman needs to dip below, it has a bubble of air trapped around its body that it uses like a diving bell!

It looks like a stick, is as long as a stick, and lives in forests full of sticks. Stretching as far as 22 inches (56 centimeters), stick insects are the longest insects on Earth. To complete its disguise, this **inconspicuous** insect may even have body parts that resemble tree buds!

 **inconspicuous** (in-kuhn-SPIK-yoo-uhs): cannot be seen easily or does not attract attention

Memory Game

Look at the pictures. What do you remember reading on the pages where each image appeared?

Index

After Reading Questions

1. How do cockroaches defend themselves against jewel wasps?
2. How many insect species have scientists identified?
3. Why does an assassin bug pile dead ants on its back?
4. How do herder ants get honeydew from aphids?
5. What's the world's longest insect?

Activity

Spend some time outdoors. List the different types of insects you can spot. Then think of ways these insects are useful to people. Do they help crops and plants grow? Are they a source of food or other raw material?

About the Author

Gary Sprott is a writer in Tampa, Florida. He's not too squeamish about creepy-crawlies. Except earwigs! Those little horrors give him the heebie-jeebies.

www.rourkeeducationalmedia.com

PHOTO CREDITS: Cover: ©Andrey Pavlov, ©wwing; Pg 11 & 30 ©Neil Bromhall; Pg 12 & 30 © Adriana Margarita Larios Arellano; Pg 15 & 30 ©CreativeNature_nl; Pg 28 & 30 ©Keith Szafranski; Pg 6 & 30 © kurt_G; Pg 8 & 30 ©nechaevkon; Pg 3 ©wwing; Pg 4 ©Kevin Wells; Pg 5 ©DavidCallan; Pg 7 ©Aldemar Bernal; Pg 9 ©Amitrane; Pg 11 ©gan chaonan; Pg 13 ©rainbow-7; Pg 14 ©Lakeview Images; Pg 16-17 ©Oleg Znamenskiy; Pg 17 ©PK6289; Pg 18 ©saraTM; Pg 19 ©Andrei310; Pg 19 ©webguzs; Pg 20 ©webguzs; Pg 21 ©Jean Landry; Pg 22 ©Adisak Mitrprayoon; Pg 23 ©Alex25; Pg 23 ©Jean Landry; Pg 25 ©Jean Landry; Pg 26 ©phototrip; Pg 26-27 ©MikeLane45

Edited by: Kim Thompson
Cover and Interior design by: Kathy Walsh

Library of Congress PCN Data

Ants Are Farmers! And Other Strange Facts / Gary Sprott
(That's Wild!)
  ISBN 978-1-73161-729-3 (hardcover)
  ISBN 978-1-73161-253-3 (softcover)
  ISBN 978-1-73161-741-5 (e-Book)
  ISBN 978-1-73161-753-8 (ePub)
Library of Congress Control Number: 2019932379

Rourke Educational Media
Printed in the United States of America,
North Mankato, Minnesota